The Pimp-A-Lo Syndrome. . . .

The Cross Between a Pimp and a Gigalo. . . .

Volume 1

E. Teena Harris

Table of Contents

Foreword

Yes, I am a female writing about the "pimp" mentality & the "gigalo" syndrome. If you picked up this book perhaps you experienced the pimp or gigalo mentality, or you have some level of interest in this subject matter because you have been pimped or played; or seen it happen to someone. I wrote this book with the intention to expose the game and agony of this syndrome; not to condone the behavior. Nevertheless, I wanted to share my experience of falling in love with someone who was a cross between a pimp and a gigalo, better as known as Pimp-A-Lo. This book is intended to reveal and challenge the belief system that society values about the "pimpin" mentality. With my words, I believe that I can expose the truth and save lives from becoming victimized by their own ill intentions.

My Story

In an effort to protect the person involved some aspects will be adjusted. However, lies will not be told because in order to provide an accurate account of events "my truth" must be stated. Also, I do not want to draw attention to the individual involved, but I want to draw attention to the behavior.

I was in a vulnerable place due to a personal catastrophe that occurred in my life, the murder of a family member. During this time I was broken, confused, and angry with God about the loss that happened in my family. I was in need of serious help; and I was keenly aware of it. I reached out to supportive friends, to gain emotional support and they connected me with a support person to assist me that I did not know. It was a referral from an acquaintance that I had known for 14 years. Being that I was traumatized and out of touch with my own reality the support person, I was referred to became my rescuer or so I thought.

My Rescuer (Drama Triangle) assisted me with the immediate emotional support I desperately needed at that time, and he also told me that I was going to be his future wife. At the time, I didn't believe him, but he was very kind and extremely attractive and highly educated. He also had a sense of humor that distracted me from the gut-wrenching pain that I was experiencing from my traumatic grief. He was also very emotionally vulnerable with me & highly knowledgeable about women's issues & overcoming serious hardships due to his own experiences in life. This piqued my interest and caused me to draw closer to him emotionally.

For several days we hung out, ate dinner, talked intimately about life, and had fun together; with no sex involved; and then I went back home. I was out of town when I met this individual. He maintained contact with me, telling me all the things that any woman would love to hear. I was still vulnerable, traumatized, attending murder trials, and attracted to him & celibate for a number of years. The more we talked, the more emotionally tied I became to this individual.

He later invited me to an event to see him, at an event out of town that I had not planned on attending, but he persisted. He even went as far to use our "shared acquaintance" that introduced us, to talk me into coming. So, I went to this event to see him and close friends at this special event. During the course of our time together, on this trip, we broke my years of celibacy, and I become more connected with this man. After this seemingly wonderful time he began to evade the relationship, and I continued to ask why. I did not understand how we could get so close, cross the line that we thoroughly discussed that we were crossing, and he just disappeared like that! My gear continued to shift from grief to trauma, and I believed that I should fight for us because perhaps he was afraid of the real thing in a relationship. I continued communication intermittently letting him know that I was there for him because I knew he had some serious issues from things he shared with me about himself; that I will not disclose. I wanted to rescue him (Drama Triangle) because he had done so with me. Subconsciously, I believed I owed him something for assisting with saving my life during such a traumatic period, unbeknownst to me at the time.

A lengthy amount of time goes by and he finally surfaced. When he came back, he had a story as to why he evaded the relationship, and I fell for it. He and I continued to communicate and then one day he contacted me in crisis. He told me about a legal matter that he needed my help with. Now here I am a trained Clinical Counselor that deals with crisis for a living, surely I can help him-right?!? Wrong!!!

I assisted him financially with his dilemma and he was supposed to pay me back. He started to visit me and we spent beautiful weekends and days full of making love, laughing, going out to eat, going to movies, deep intimate talks at bedtime, and all at my expense. He had made unhealthy choices with his finances before he met me that led to the current "drama triangle" we were in. I accepted him right where he was at: Handsome, educated, financially broke, spiritually broken, health issues, and with a "story" and a "promise" of working through these things with me because we were going to get married one day; that was our plan. Over months he continued to have numerous crises financially, and he was always asking me for money for his children that I loved vicariously through him. He asked for money for his car, rent, food, and gas. I continued to make suggestions to him about ways to be more responsible and then he would; get an attitude, ignore me, or tell me that he knew all of that stuff already because he had multiple degrees and had it going on in the past he was just having a rough time in his life.

After all the support I gave him, he cheated on me with another woman and it came out on Facebook. In disbelief, I thought the man I knew was actually trying to better himself by gaining employment as a professor at the university in my city but instead he was breaking my heart. The pain settled on my heart like tons of bricks and this happened right before my birthday. He was living his life and I was suffering in silence.

I was in a position, with the help of a special group of friends to take an honest inventory of the entire relationship, which I did not like, but it was gravely needed. This special group of friends assisted me with looking at: Who he told me he was in the past- a womanizer, how he always took advantage of situations even if the situation was not financial, and that he had no integrity in the past. They also assisted me with examining the multiple times he would emotionally abandon the relationship & only resurface when he needed something ,and that he was only proving to be a burden in my life and a user, and that he never loved me for being me, but that he loved the benefits that came with me. Of course, I didn't want to hear that I barked at the thought that someone would get that close to me, and stab me in the back like that! I was in denial! I had been hood-winked, bam-boozled, and I bought the dream and story he sold. I was crushed. I gave this man my time, spirit, and body that I valued. Not to mention, I loaned him money and I had never given any man money before in my life, never was asked to, nor volunteered to do so. I was a legitimate "first-timer". The money I loaned and on a few occasions I gave wasn't chump change! We are talking thousands of dollars.

Some people may wonder, "Why would she do all of that when a man told her about his past?" I am glad that you asked. In various healing communities it is very common for the persons that attend them to have issues and be actively working on these issues, and they do become better people. I participate in one of these healing communities and so did my Pimp-A-Lo. It is common for people in these healing communities to have colorful past and change. I did, and so have millions of others. I believed that this was going to be the case here, but it was not. Additionally, my Pimp-A-Lo had a unique health issue that was similar to my Father's, who died in 2006, and it triggered my grief. I am a Daddy's girl and I loved my Father very much. There were times when my Pimp-A-Lo had a health scare that reminded me of my Father, whom I took care of daily, along with other family member's, until he died. When my Pimp-A-Lo had this similar issue too, sometimes I would see my father instead of my Pimp-A-Lo. Ongoing inventory work assisted me with seeing this. However, while I was in it I did not see it clearly. Ultimately, my experience with my Pimp-A-Lo triggered much unfinished business that I had in relation to: Unaddressed grief issues, care-taking issues, and codependency issues. So, this experience was a PAINFUL lesson & BLESSING in disguise. It was guided help turned backwards; that's what trauma will do to if left unchecked, or one believes that it has been fully checked and it has not. For the record, often times one does not know if they have gotten better with an issue until they are presented with it!

My "EXCRUCIATING" healing process began, and I started to do the work on my poor boundary setting, emotional abuse issues, and the codependency that set me up for accepting this chaos & bull in my life. As a trained clinical professional, it didn't dawn on me: 1. Never make major decisions in your first year of traumatic grief, 2. Look for evidence and not promises or excuses. Since I improperly diagnosed myself—I became a candidate for the very same people that God uses me to help on a daily basis; without judgment of those I serve I state this. I realized that I was in school again; emotional maturity school and I did not like attending this school!

Over a period of months of crying, hurting, getting angry, still worrying about him, and needing help myself I began to get a revelation. The revelation came to me after I fell in love with this man; spent thousands of dollars helping him; and I couldn't get as much as a phone call back or a text message. One morning I had a revelation that he was not just a user, a pimp, or a gigalo he was a Pimp-A-Lo. I came to the painful conclusion that I couldn't love this man out of this "deeply ingrained" mentality that he had of using women and people; along with his family-of-origin issues. I knew enough about his history, by this time, that the women in his life always took care of him because of: his looks, charisma, stories he sold, and sexual abilities. He told me he had pimped hoes in his past, womanized, and believed in various sexual practices, but that he had changed because of his need to change spiritually. However, I never saw the change, it was an illusion. I only held on to the hope of him changing, and I had help in holding on to the hope of this man changing from people who: Were incapable of participating in their own rescue; and had male-codependency issues themselves. So, it dawned on me, "You have fallen in love with a pimp-a-lo, and you will need some divine and therapeutic help to break free from this cycle". Now some may be judging, and that is fine, because if my story helps somebody from falling "prey" to the "pimp-a-lo syndrome" it was well worth it. Out of this dynamic, as previously mentioned, I learned about Dr. Stephen Karpman's "Drama Triangle". In this triangle there are three roles: Rescuer, Persecutor, and Victim. There is a way to break this triangle that we will discuss further in chapter 7.

So let's dig a little deeper into my discovery of: The Pimp-A-Lo Syndrome . . .

What is a Pimp?

In the most obvious sense of the word, most will exclaim, "I know what a pimp is!!" Perhaps, they do, but I want to offer another perspective on what being a pimp is. Now the Urban Dictionary states, "A Pimp is: P. Person I. Into M. Marketing P. Prostitutes. One who brokers the sexual favors of women for profits?" However, there are aspects of "pimping" that are not highlighted in this definition. Now this perspective is raw, but as I have heard it eloquently put before, "Its tight, but its right!" Pimps take care of their prostitutes. They make sure their hoe's have: Make-up, clothing, pap-smears, condoms, and physical protection. Also, pimps ensure that their prostitutes or hoes have a proper emotional mentality to handle business, and if they don't the pimps take the time to get their hoe's in line, because ultimately if they are unstable and not properly presented they are bad for business. It's a waste of the investment on both ends; and a real pimp can't stand to lose money, so he must "train" his prostitutes. Real pimps are sold out on image and producing quality product to keep customers coming. **In other words, pimping goes far beyond the sex game-it's a mentality that can be used on women or men that are NOT prostitutes or male-whores.** For instance, a car sales man can be a pimp. He wants to ensure that the lot looks appealing, the grounds are kept, and the cars are clean. Even though, the cars maybe **"lemons"** he wants the cars to look like **"diamonds"**. The same is true for a dishonest real estate agent; any property that he or she presents they must: Know the value of the property, understand what is truly needed for maintenance, and how to present it to a potential buyer even if they know the property is worthless.

The common theme here with the traditional pimp, car salesman, and real estate agent is: **Power (or the appearance of power), knowledge, money, ego, perception, and manipulation.** Moreover; we have many want-to-be pimps that are not filling the requirements for "pimping" on a fundamental level. We have pimps that do not maintain their prostitutes make sure their needs are met, but yet they expect to be paid with no investment on their part. This theory also applies to the fraudulent car salesman's that doesn't take the initiative to maintenance his inventory but yet they are upset when they do not sell any cars. Lastly, we have the real estate pimp, who does not do any research on the property, upkeep, or the presentation on the land, but yet they want to sell a house or a condo. Which brings us to another common theme with these pimps, none of them want to put in any work, but want the fringe benefits of obtaining a score, or a sale. This is how come the dating game is so messed up today. We have phony pimps that are role-playing being "real pimps" that are lazy, shiftless, and do not take care of their product (whatever the product may be). Then the product begins to live the "illusion" of them being a thorough-bread, but they are fraudulent. There is nothing worse than a broke-down pimp that thinks he is Hue Hefner, Playboy founder, or Mike Lowery from Bad Boys II, when he is not. However, if this is the role that you want to portray it is your choice, but let me offer you some advice.

1. Spend quality time with "real pimps" and allow them to provide you with the tutelage to become one.
2. Study any and all material on being a real pimp, and a successful one at that.
3. Don't switch lanes, stay true to the "game" or "lane" of being a pimp. Don't sell any dreams that you know that you cannot fulfill nor have any intentions fulfilling.

These three suggestions may assist you with not having to experience the following consequences: **Head being** cracked to the white meat (suggestion: physical abuse), disturbing appearances or calls to your job, tires being slashed, windows busted out, sugar in your tank, harassing phone calls, PPO (protective orders of engagement), loss of respect including family& your own children, and the ultimate a broken heart & spirit that cannot be easily repaired. These are things that are potential consequences that may be irreversible not only to the "prostituted" but to the "want-to-be pimp" as well; not to mention S.T.D.'s that are incurable & "PRISON" time.

Are you a real pimp? A pretending pimp? Is pimping so attractive now? I'm just saying . . .

What is a Gigalo?

The word gigalo sounds appealing. However, its meaning is atrocious as we dissect it. The Urban dictionary classifies a gigalo as: A man hoe . . . Male who is paid by women to have sex with. Prostitute, whore; the male version of whore. Now, this word, just like the word "pimp", has deeper implications that we are going to address. We are going to examine three types of gigalo's. **The High Dollar Gigalo, The Low-Budget Gigalo, and The Down on His Luck Gigalo**.

High Dollar Gigalo: For example, a well off financially independent woman may decide to hire a male-escort to take her to a function or an office dinner party. As a part of this package the gigalo is become her arm trophy, cater to her, and after the event provides sexual pleasures to her liking. He does all of this at a set fee, with no negotiations. She clearly understands what services she is paying for and she expects top notch performance in any & all domains that he is to fulfill during the evening. He is apprised of this expectation and he examines the roles that she wants played, and he ensures that he studies her enough so that he may get paid and paid properly! As a matter of fact, he gets a bonus if he provides a stellar performance in her eyes. He is also usually educated and well-rounded. He brings a lot to the table; he expects more and he knows he must give more.

Ultimately, the high dollar gigalo does the following things for a woman that hires him: 1. Holds her, 2. Opens the door for her, 3. Sexual and Intimate fantasies fulfilled, 4. An emotional ear piece if she wants one5. Stimulating intellectual conversations. These are just some real basic functions of a high dollar gigalo. An **"expert"** high dollar gigalo is well studied at the craft of catering to a woman's needs, he is well trained that he can get her to throw in extra amenities that she was not even bargaining for because his mouth piece has so much **"swag"** that she will buy the anything to please him. For example: Trips out state, a new leisure Suit, new Gators, and even a Rolex watch instead of a Timex. This is an **expert high dollar gigalo**, and she is not upset at his behavior because he has done everything she purchased and more. If he get a little out of line she can tolerate him because she knows what to expect from him, and he has more than enough **"feigned emotional**

compassion" to iron out any and all misunderstandings that could potentially arise. Now we go to the low budget gigalo.

Low-Budget Gigalo: However, there are low budget mentality gigalo's that are not effective, nor on the job appropriately. At this time we are about to undercut and expose the low-budget tacky gigalo's that are currently in the game-messing it up for everybody else. This type of gigalo is attracted to welfare queens and hood-rats. **While these terms are slang terms meant to label and degrade women, especially women in the African-American community, they are common and most can relate to the stigma that comes with these terms. I am not endorsing these terms or in support of degrading my sisters of all races out there. I am just merely stating that these terms are used in reference to what the low-budget gigalo are attracted to by definition through research.** Low-Budget Gigalo's low expectations and this type of gigalo looks for women that can provide him with basic living necessities (food stamps, and use of her E.B.T. card for cleaning supplies, boxers, or sneakers). The low budget gigalo becomes a professional baby daddy (meaning he has more than one child by multiple women) and they find women that are willing to have their baby, so that they may end up living off of the "baby-momma." Typically, low budget gigalo's are from the inner city and usually, **not always**, come from single parent households where the female was the predominate figure. These types of gigalo's are used to dominating & hard working-women like their mother or auntie, whom have taken care of them. They may seek a mother/child relationship with their **"female targets"**. Since these guys have no tight game and low self-esteem because if they did they would not live in low-income housing with their women, or need their welfare supplements. They rely on great sex and their looks to obtain as a bargaining tool. These low budget gigalo's will borrow the woman's car, tell the woman to buy them clothes, buy games for their **X-BOXES**, and any other item that they can get. Moreover, the ironic thing about low budget gigalos is that they **"LOVE"** to go around **"BRAGGING"** to others about, **"How much big pimping that they are doing!"** This is a sad state of affairs; and this type of gigalo will do anything, and I do mean anything, to get his needs met at the woman's expense! His internal rationale for this behavior is that," She is just collateral damage if anything occurs that he is responsible for." Lastly, we have the "Down on his luck Gigalo".

<u>Down on His Luck Gigalo:</u> This type of gigalo likes to use a **sympathetic approach** on his female targets. He targets square women (usually stable women who are not into games and they are spiritual). These women typically fall into his age group or a little younger, and he will come into her life with a gentle manly approach as if he is together, or he is trying to get himself together. This is the **most dangerous** of the three gigalos' because he **once** had it "**going on**" and he is on the **prowl** to get back on the top of the game by any means necessary. The Down on His Luck Gigalo is a "**Legend**" in his own mind and perhaps within certain communities" **Once he gets his foot in the door he will conveniently: Lose his job, get his car in the shop, have baby- mother issues, legal problems, etc . . .** When the woman he is dealing with sees or does not see the evidence of these things occurring because she is already emotionally invested. He is attractive and a **"master manipulator"**. She will do everything in **her power**, and **beyond her power** to **"help him"**. He becomes her full-time job with no benefits. He is "keenly" aware that she is going to help him because he is relying on her maternal instincts to achieve his own agenda. The down on his luck gigalo is a "MASTER" in getting females to "invest" in "one" of his "alleged" dreams in which he knows will "NEVER" pay off. The down on his luck gigalo doesn't bring the same money to the table as the high dollar gigalo, The down on his luck gigalo focuses on young ladies on welfare or with square jobs and these young ladies don't have the income to withhold the down on his luck gigalo, so he leaves her high and dry and heartbroken after he swindles her out of all that she does have. This guy makes her believe it was her fault, and he is now the **"victim"** because he is down on his luck and she should understand this! He places her in a vulnerable position, and again she is usually 5 to 10 years younger than him, he prefers her to be younger because out of **immaturity (and the sincere belief that he will get there with her help)** she will be easier to mold into what he wants. **If you are a gigalo stay in your lane and learn from the three category types of gigalos that proceeded before you; don't portray any other role. Don't say things like: I love you, I am down for you, and I got your back. Also It's me and you against the world, or we are getting married (mind you with no ring and no foreseeable evidence of marriage in the near future).Parenthetically, if he does marry you what are you getting? Is he equally yoked enough to even be your spouse? Will he bring joy to a marriage or just continue to use you and be a "single-husband" sleeping around while legally married to you?**

Which level of the gigalo are you and do you desire becoming a gigalo? If you still want to become one of the three gigalo's, here are some suggestions that will prove to assist you in not experiencing these consequences: **Death out of rage, true loss of the ability to experience true love in life, labeled womanizer and when you find the one you love you will lose her, extreme painful loneliness, self-hatred, enormous child-support payments that could send you to jail if not paid, spiritual death, loss** of respect from family and friends, no payment on your services, disease, and no one will want you no matter how good your sex or looks are, you will become a derelict. Eventually, you will become the person who cries wolf and nobody will come and you will be eaten alive. Possibly ending up actively addicted to using chemical substances to cope with your inner pain and never find relief.

What Is a Pimp-A-Lo; How Do They Come About?

There are many psycho-analytical reasons that I could say about what creates a Pimp-A-Lo, which is a cross between a pimp and a gigalo. However, one perspective that I will offer is: **A Pimp-A-Lo is a man who has a pimp mentality with gigalo tendencies but is not dedicated to either aspect of the roles. A Pimp-A-Lo is a very confused, insecure; man who believes that he will gain his self-worth through utilizing women to fulfill the emotional & spiritual void that he feels. He is an empty person running on "image only". Women are viewed as accomplices and targets to him.** Since he is **not** accustomed to having authentic relationships, he will sabotage every authentic relationship that comes into his life. **A**

<u>**Pimp-A-Lo is a man without a sense of true purpose and he wanders in and out of people's lives (a nomad of sorts) creating havoc and chaos unbeknownst or knowingly to him.**</u> This is a man that is "void of a true spiritual connection" that ties one to the beauty and appreciation of life. Due to his ability to be charismatic, witty, funny, educated, and perhaps a great physical lover he is not easily detected, and **probably** does not realize the nature of his condition; especially if he has played this role for a very long time! He knows nothing else to do but play the game! <u>**The Pimp-A-Lo has VERY STRONG CHARACTERISTICS of a SOCIOPATH.**</u> **This is a man on fire, full of resentment, regret, and broken dreams and he cannot see the forest for the trees, or wake up and smell the coffee simply because he is:** Loved, appreciated, recognized, or supported by people that mean him well in his life. **These things are not enough for the Pimp-A-Lo.** Only a true and sincere prayer from the Pimp-A-Lo himself, or someone, perhaps his mother or other person and "his personal surrender to God" will assist this "half of a man" with hitting the bottom of himself, to find the beginning of a loving, caring, God that can **help him too**; and ladies we are not it!!! To make it more plain, **"YOU ARE NOT HIS GOD"**

Ladies, make no mistake about it there is **ABSOLUTELY** nothing you can do: Sex, cooking, changing your weave, giving him money, getting breast implants, nose jobs, taking your vagina-up, going to the Pastor, or series of relationship workshops in any domain that will change the pimp-a-lo. Aforementioned actions of a Pimp-A-Lo are misinterpreted as, "I got game, I got her, and here we go again." He will totally misread your well-intended manipulations to **"get him to change"**, and blame **"you"** for his continued inability to stand and be the man that the Lord created! ***The reason he does this again is because he is confused and emotionally/ spiritually ill.*** Your actions of trying to help the Pimp-A-Lo, will further perpetuate his unhealthy cycle. In other words, you are doing the same things for him that many others before you have done, and they have failed. So, while what you are doing to try and **"help him"** seems unique, and you believe it will show him **"something different"** it is in fact showing him: **The same movie 25 times over. Basically, you are merely the "new character" in a soap opera that has been going on with him for "years".**

Ultimately, if you continue to **use religion** and other **self-help philosophies** that come from fly by night professionals you will become **"lost"**. Your identity will become that of the Pimp-A-Lo, and *"you will" experience:* **Low self-worth, low-self-esteem, distrust of trustworthy people that mean you well, hostility, and an insurmountable defense wall that will keep anything good from coming into your life.** While this may seem harsh, it needs to be said, and stated plainly. Additionally, I am speaking this from my own personal experience and the experience of many women that I have worked with clinically and spiritually. In all honesty, my healing process remains ongoing for me since I fell in love and lust with a pimp-a-lo.

Many women will use scriptures to justify remaining in "unacceptable conditions" with their male counterparts saying things like, "God is going to work it out. I am praying for Him. What God put together let no man tear it apart." Not only do we use religion to justify the most outrageous sort of non-sense, we will start attacking other women, and healthy men friends in our lives by saying things such as: <u>**"You hating on me. You in my business, What about when you was doing this, that, and the third, so who are you to tell me what to do about my pimp-a-lo?"**</u> While this may seem extreme, it is a true reality that we see every day of our lives if we pay close enough attention. Then our female egos will tell us, when the Pimp-A-Lo leaves us hanging high and dry, **<u>because that's what he does,</u>** that some wonderful man left us when really **<u>"King Kong" left us!</u>** The Pimp-A-Lo wasn't a man of substance, integrity, and character. He's a nightmare!!! We will begin to come a loose at the seams, fall out crying, check ourselves into mental institutions, perhaps start using chemical substances, and keep people on the phone for hours on end about what the Pimp-A-Lo is doing **"this time"**. However, he has been doing it and it's time for us to stand up and be real women. **STOP** harming ourselves and these brothers that are already wounded, broken, and confused. Please take off your <u>**Wonder Woman Capes**</u>, and stop trying to save an "Adult Male" from the experience of becoming a "Grown Man". _**These pimp-a-lo's will NEVER**_ _**stop behaving in the manner that they do, until we stop**_ _**supporting it.**_ If you really love your pimp-a-lo, and more importantly yourself, "DON'T" help him!!!!!! **Love your-** **self and him enough to LET GO and LET GOD work** **on him!**

 <u>**Next time do the following:**</u> Let his car break down, do not give him money or food stamps, do not have sex with him, do not bail him out of jail let him go to jail, and most certainly DO NOT move him into your house whether you are on Section 8 or you're a home owner. If he is on his mother's couch leave him on her couch and refuse to date him until he obtains gainful employment **make him work** **for you and your time, after all you are worth it!** For the truth be told many pimp-a-lo's have mother's, auntie's, sister's, or female cousins that keep them from developing emotionally into men and assists them with remaining **"seasoned teenagers"** even if they are over 30 years of age or higher. Also, some of these Pimp-A-Lo's have their own apartment or house but they depend on their mother's. In other words, they have a **covert emotional incestuous** rela-tionship with their mother's (or Auntie's that raised them

some female figure) that keeps them from loving ANY other woman completely or the way that she deserves to be loved. He also short changes himself, but he does not see it. He thinks its game!

So, the last thing he needs is for us, as women, to become another caretaker. Let the truth be told, he will lose respect for you because while most women think, "I ride or die for my man . . ." they forget that this statement applies to a real man; that does the same for her! **In other words, a Pimp-A-Lo is NOT a real man so this statement cannot apply to him!** The Pimp-A-Lo will interpret your "help-ride or die syndrome" as, "She is a shaky, insecure, depressed woman who doesn't mind allowing a man to take "full advantage" of her! She is a dam fool and I got her." How do I know this because I have experienced it and hundreds of other women have too, and beyond my personal experience I have **"interviewed" real pimps, gigalo's, and real men, and this is what they say about this kind of behavior.**

I know, I know, and I know, this is a hard-pill to swallow, but it is necessary if we are to get men back in the homes being real men and also for us to regain the lost identity that we have as women that play multiple roles. **Let me suggest to every woman reading this book to find you a male mentor that you are "NOT" sexually attracted to that is balanced emotionally, spiritually, and financially and run your thoughts, ideas, and behaviors past him**

"BEFORE" you act. Keep in mind that men DO NOT think like we do and they do not operate like we do. We can talk to our girlfriends about men, our mothers, and everyone else but you need a man's perspective on what to basically expect out of a man. Also, don't limit yourself to whom you speak to, if you can interview some former pimps, or players, or gigalo's ask them about the game and let them tell you first-hand, and be prepared for some real talk. You may want to take a pen, pencil, laptop, or any mechanism to take notes on, because some of these men will educate you. If you are afraid get on the buddy system. **In other words, if you are vulnerable and think you might get "broke off" trying to get some information, take someone else along with you for the interview.** After all, you have taken yourself through enough.

A Pimp-A-Lo while skillfully a master of manipulation always requires a **WILLING VESSEL**, so we must take responsibility for: **The part we played with the pimp-a-lo's**. At the end of the day women have always played a major role, if not the primary role in the creation of a Pimp-A-Lo. Examples are: Bonnie &Clyde, Ride or Die, Captain-Save-A-Ho Syndromes, and Stand By Your Man attitudes and beliefs. Most women and men to have **learned** "these behaviors. However, the hope shot is just as you learned it you can **"unlearn"** it; and begin to live a full life that you were originally intended to live.

Be True To Your To Your Selected Role

This small chapter speaks directly to three things: Your role, Transparency, and Personal Choice. When I speak of being true to your role, I am speaking to who you are portraying. In other words, if you are a pimp say you are a pimp. If you are a gigalo say you are a gigalo and if you are a Pimp-A-Lo lover say your one. Essentially, I am speaking to being as transparent as possible concerning "who you are" when interacting with others. While you maybe a little confused, we all have some basic pre-tense on "who we are" and the "types of things" that we do or that we like. We can even make it simpler, we know what we are attracted to . . . **It's important to know what hooks you! For instance, a sympathetic story with a promise of change "used" to hook me.** Once you establish your role be transparent about it in other words tell the truth. Don't lie, don't role-play;

just be for real. Operating in this matter will not **beguile**
or **manipulate**. You have not **robbed** somebody of their
choice. Some people will tell you who they are only in an
effort to draw you in emotionally and they have a hidden
agenda the entire time. They will use a line similar to this,
"I told you who I was, and now you want you act like
this . . ." We're not talking about this kind of transparency
here!!! So, that you won't fall for this one, when a person
"tells you" who they are BELIEVE them!!!!! Right at that
very moment start "examining their actions and inactions.
Truthfully enough, inactions speak louder than any words
ever spoken. In other words, "silence is loud". Che Gavana
once stated, "Silence is argument carried out by other
means . . ." If the person says nothing they have said plenty
& shown you plenty enough evidence!!! When staying true
to the role presents itself start a written or mental inventory
which ever works best for you.

Also, obtain some **Accountability Partners** that participate in their own rescue. Meaning: ***"They are rela-***
tively healthy & working on their own issues & you can
see good fruit from their lives". Allow these persons to
become "FULLY AWARE" of your short-comings, and
use them as your eyes and ears because you will need it.
Additionally, they can help you not become Cinderella,
Alice in Wonderland, or any other fictional character in
a non-fiction fairy tale. **The bottom line here is come to**

know **"YOU"** and stay in your own lane. Some of us hide behind: Our titles at work, in the church, roles as mentor's or guides in various communities etcetera, yet we do not know who we are. Start inventorying you right away, and in this manner you will be **"less likely"** to get **"played"**.

I know, I know, I know, (hands on your hips attitude out cold) you are not about to be played again, you know the game!!!! Hear me when I say this, *"As long as we are on this side of heaven there are some games that we do not know, and we can all be played".* I have learned that the hard way from my "personal experience". As a matter of fact, there was once a song by Teddy Pendergrass titled, "The Whole Town's Laughing At Me" . . . In the song he is speaking about being played and being made a fool out of but he thought he had a "handle" on the love. He went on to make another record, perhaps not in this order, but he made it nonetheless, and the name of the song was, "Love T.K.O". In this song he continued to repeat one line, "I think I better let it go . . . looks like another love T.K.O." Now, I don't about you; reader but this sister has absolutely no interest in the whole town laughing at me again, and experiencing another love T.K.O. (**technical knock-out**). I would much rather know who I am, what I like, what hooks me, what are my tendencies, and take a regular inventory (many inventories are available you may request of me at a later date) before I hop out there and fall in love with another pimp-a-lo. One thing is for certain about history, it always repeats itself unless different action takes place in present time to alter historical repetition. *For the most part, if it's in your history to deal with the "pimp-a-lo" type you have a stronger bending toward doing it again, if you don't learn to be in your reality and deal with your intrapersonal issues.*

Breaking Free From A Pimp-A-Lo

At this point, you may be feeling: Enraged, annoyed, bitter, sad, frustrated, deceitful, defeated, unhappy, or unsure about what to do concerning your Pimp-A-lo, or a loved one that you now know is "caught in the grip" with a Pimp-A-Lo. From the onset, let me say this, it is NOT my intention to "shame" you, but IT IS my intention to arouse and provoke thought within you, to do something DIFFERENTLY, so that you will stop harming yourself, him & others that love you & see you **destroying yourself.** Make no mistake about it, others get harmed too when they walk through this with you & then you go back time and time again & fall-out with them for trying to help you. *The behavior that takes in this dynamic of the "Pimp-A-Lo syndrome is like that of the "Domestic Violence Wheel of Power & Control"*

The first step to breaking free from the "Pimp-A-Lo Syndrome" is to properly diagnose it for what it really is. In other words, get HONEST with yourself about what has really been going on with you and this "adult male" who is NOT a "grown man" just because he is of age legally, meaning over 18years old. Your Pimp-A-Lo may be in his: 20's, 30's, 40's, and yes even his 50's. This is easily assessed when you examine **your behavior** in relation to all that was mentioned in the previous chapters.

After, you assess and diagnose the problem correctly then you can "begin" the process of breaking free from this **DEVESTATING Syndrome.** One of the things that have proven to be most helpful to me in my breaking free (and notice I said break "in" present tense) has been: The Stephen Karpman's Drama Triangle. In this triangle are three major roles that are tied to codependency, and I will explain it below.

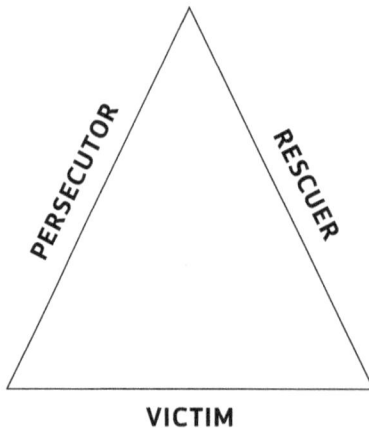

PERSECUTOR   RESCUER

VICTIM

The bottom side of this triangle is the "VICTIM" the bottom left corner is the "PERSECUTOR" and the top is the "RESCUER". Historically, these developments on "manipulation games" were first introduced in the 1950's decade. Eric Berne is credited for initially founding a major aspect of this theory and he wrote a book, "Games People Play Ballantine Books (Toronto, 1973). So, let's take a look at "3" hypothetical play outs of this triangle because it is so complicated that is it perplexing, but yet understandable at the same time.

Hypothetical Scenario 1: There is a woman who is being beaten by her husband, so the neighbors call the police. At this time the "wife" is the "VICTIM" and the husband is the "PERSECUTOR" So, now the policeman comes and he is the "RESCUER/SAVIOR". The policeman enter the home, places the husband on the ground, and now Policeman is the "PERSECUTOR", the husband is the "VICTIM" and the wife is now the "SAVIOR/RESCUER" when she begins to plead, argue, and defend her husband's actions to the police. Saying, "Don't hurt him, he didn't mean it". Notice how the wife went from being the "VICTIM" to the "RESCUER/SAVIOR" in a matter of moments, but in **one scene**. In actual fact, these roles are interchangeable and a person can become all three *"very quickly"* it is an emotional and sometimes physically abusive triangle.

Hypothetical Scenario 2: John Doe is dating Jane Doe, and John cheats on Jane and they have a fight about his indiscretion. Jane is now the "VICTIM" and John is the "PERSECUTOR". A month passes and the girl Janice Doe that John cheated on Jane with is pregnant by John. So, now a heated emotional argument occurs between John, Jane, and Janice Doe. This argument has turned into an altercation and now all three of them are in court facing charges. John is now the "VICTIM" Janice is now the "PERSECUTOR" and Jane is now the "SAVIOR". Jane is in court "supporting" her man and Janice Doe is the problem, not John & his cheating and Jane allowing it and accepting it. So, this melodrama plays out on an ongoing basis as long as John and Jane are together well after Janice Doe has the baby & they leave court, and by the way it is John's baby for real, and Jane is now the "VICTIM" again and becomes a **"nag"** to John each time she brings up Janice Doe and their baby, and Janice Doe (the baby mother) is always the "problem and the persecuted", never John, or Jane for continuing to participate. So, now Jane has assumed a role of **"permanent victim"**.

Hypothetical Scenario 3: John Doe is in a financial crisis, so he claims, and he goes to his woman Jane Doe to bail him out. John is the "VICTIM" and Jane is the "SAVIOR" after Jane helps John out of his **umpteenth financial crisis** because she is his, woman his, "Ride or die chick" they may be married, engaged, or they have been together for years." John Doe becomes irritated with Jane Doe when she begins to question him about his irresponsibility, committing to her & "their dreams", and getting business in order. Now John Doe has turned into the "Persecutor" of Jane Doe, who is "helping" him & Jane Doe is both the "VICTIM and RESCUER/SAVIOR" because of her investment into John Doe. Also, Jane Doe feels obligated to always support John Doe or else, he will leave, so now she is in emotional and financial bondage and John Doe is in the power position of "PERSECUTOR" and threatens to leave at the drop of a dime because he KNOWS that Jane Doe will do **anything for him**, because her patterns have **proven** that she will. At this point, Jane Doe will think she is in love, when in fact she is in a dysfunctional abusive triangle **drenched** with "codependency". Victims always wonder, and or state, *"Why does this keep happening to me?"* Victims may also say things like, *"I am going to work with my man I will be dam if I put all of this work into him & some other woman ends up getting the benefits!"* The Victim is truly in denial & refusal because there are no benefits that are worth one's emotional sanity & spiritual wellness!

The point here in all three hypothetical scenarios is the "roles" that the people in them play. This can also apply with a mother's rescuing a son; father's rescuing a daughter, and so on. Ultimately, the triangle is based on codependency and "layers" of manipulation that are harmful. So the million dollar question is, **"HOW DO I BREAK FREE FROM THIS MADNESS".** I am glad that you asked ☺

Step One: If one of the roles changes the whole triangle base is weakened. In other words, if a Victim becomes empowered and stops rescuing then the Persecution and Rescuer roles will not have any juice. So, if you are in this triangle you want to move to the center of the drama triangle by NOT participating. Stand your ground become very sensitive to what is occurring in your scenario.

Step Two: The other suggestion for breaking the triangle is to REFUSE your opponents force! Don't give in to their demands & this will halt their attacks on you to assume one of the three roles in the triangle. If this is done effectively, you saying & **displaying** a **"FIRM NO"** & refusing to "play the game", this will render your opponent (lover) "powerless", or else they will "unmask" themselves and risk exposing "the game". So one of two things will happen:

(1) They will stop talking with you, asking you for help, or communicating with you period (which may be a great thing if all they are doing is bring drama & pain in your life) or (2) They will get honest about their real motives and intentions toward you, and about themselves and begin to take responsible actions. In either case, you will create the **least harm** for you and gain peace and create the **least harm** to them by not perpetuating their dependence on you. While I realize that number 1 may be painful for you, because it was for me, sometimes it's a blessing in disguise, and one can learn to embrace the **"good"** in **"good-bye"**. If this is the case, support groups, church, therapy, family, and sound friends can help you process through your feelings, but you will be better in the end.

Step Three: If you find that you are truly, truly, struggling with *building a relationship* with the word **"NO"** and you cannot seem to break free. It is my suggestion that you seek Therapy and attend some Al-Anon or Co-Dependency meetings. Most times, this pattern is deeply rooted in one's family of origin, and **can't be** easily broken. Having this awareness is meaningless if it cannot be applied. Typically, in the Afro-American community it is unheard of to attend a Therapist because you may be considered "crazy" for going. Most of this belief is predicated upon the distrust that the Afro-American community has due to years of enslavement and other cultural beliefs. However, as an Afro-American Clinical Counselor and receiver of therapy, I would like to submit to you that, **"Going to therapy and actually "doing the work" of therapy has enhanced the quality of my life & my personal relationship with God."** So, you won't be "crazy" if you go to therapy, but you may be **"ran crazy"** if you continue in this dysfunctional cycle. As a matter of fact, this cycle is based on sheer and utter insanity. Doing the same thing over and over and over again, knowing what the results will be, but persisting on anyway. Each time "believing", "It will be different this time . . ." and it never is!!!!! It only WORSENS!!! *It will only be DIFFERENT, if you become DIFFERENT.*

Additional resources will be discussed in the closing chapter for those that desire seeking additional support in breaking free. Keep in mind that resources are **"not iron clad"** guarantees that you will break free, but may serve as a catalyst in your healing journey. These resources are available at your personal discretion to assist you. Remember: *"You are ultimately the resource that will get you free!"*

Closing Thoughts

Writing this book has been an emotional rollercoaster ride. However, it was well worth it if it helps one person to break free from this dramatic and dangerous process. Please know that I am not judging: A Pimp, Gigalo, or a Pimp-A-Lo but I am highlighting the aspects of each of these roles, and how damaging they can be to the human soul. Part 2 of this syndrome will discuss in more detail the aspects of remaining free from this syndrome through practical behavioral and spiritual responses. Please know that these spiritual responses will not arrive from a faulty theology perspective, but they will have the actual mechanics on how stay free with God's help.

Acknowledgements

I would like to thank some people that assisted me with this journey, for I would be remised not to mention them. I want to thank my friend Joe Blow & his former pimp/

gigalo associates, names that I am leaving anonymous, because they used to be a real pimp's & real gigalos. Joe Blow is now a changed man for God & he is working in the Kingdom to help those still in darkness to find the light. I want to thank my spiritual sister L.C. because she has been an instrumental part of helping me and many other women stay in "REALITY" and not be "Alice in Wonderland". Her tolerance, patience, and wisdom have been priceless. I would also like to thank my mentor Pastor Dr. D. H. for keeping me emotionally and spiritually focused during the most tumultuous time in my process. I would also like to thank my other mentor Dr. N for assisting me with seeing the "simplicity" in things. I would also like to thank Mr. O who has mentored me professionally & personally on becoming a better woman & for his limitless knowledge and wisdom on living life, and clinical paradigms with men and women. I am honored that Mr. O took the time to "guide me in the tunnel". Lastly, I would like to thank the unique 12 step members that have carried me, and taught me so much over many years to become the woman that I am today, **"A woman on the grow"** . . . Remember, *"You are only as strong as your front line."*

Resources

There is an inventory guide in development by me that you may use daily to "examine yourself" to see if you are caught up in a codependency syndrome. By conducting a regular inventory you will be able to detect if you are in "fantasy" or "reality" concerning your respective situation. Contained within my inventory guide is information for Al-Anon and Codependency information for ongoing support. *In the meantime, the aforementioned support groups are "suggestions" & they are available in predominately every State in the U.S.* Ultimately, your personal willingness to invest into you will be the greatest resource because help is available & realizing and asking for help & receiving the help is the true first step in your own healing journey. I wish you well as we travel together in our ongoing personal growth and development to become the best people we can become. **Stay tuned for my self-inventory guide and part 2 of this life work; as I will be conducting speaking engagements & taking questions that will assist me further in the development of my "Personal inventory guide for healing".**

Sincerely,

References:

Online Urban Dictionary: www.urbandictionary.com

My Family for ALWAYS supporting me I love you all, "SO BIG"

Joe Blow: Anonymous Source that lived the lifestyle of a pimp and gigalo for many years, and has written a book, and changed his life for God

L.C.: Spiritual Diva who has overcome numerous tumultuous storms; and understands walking through hell to get to heaven.

Mr. O Clinically trained professional who has worked with men of all races and cultures for over 25 years.

Pastor Dr. D.H. for Spiritual tutelage, support, and life application insights

Dr. N for Clinical insights & keeping things simple

12 Step Anonymous Members for being my rock; I love you all

www.ingramcontent.com/pod-product-compliance
Lightning Source LLC
La Vergne TN
LVHW011339080426
835513LV00006B/437